The Lessons

The Gerald Cable Book Award Series

The Lessons

Joanne Diaz

Silverfish Review Press
Eugene, Oregon

Published by

Silverfish Review Press
P.O. Box 3541
Eugene, OR 97403
www.silverfishreviewpress.com

Distributed by

Small Press Distribution
800-869-7553
spd@spdbooks.org
www.spdbooks.org

Library of Congress Cataloging-in-Publication Data

Diaz, Joanne.
  The lessons / Joanne Diaz. -- 1st ed.
      p. cm.
  ISBN 978-1-878851-59-8 (alk. paper)
  I. Title.
  PS3604.I18L47 2011
  811'.6--dc22

                        2010047682

Manufactured in the United States of America

Contents

for my family

The Lessons

Granada

To be so far from oxtail stew, sardines
in garlic sauce, blood oranges in pails
along the avenida, midday heat
wetting necks and wrists; to be so stuck
in stone-thick ice and clouds and recall
the pomegranate we shared, its hardened peel,
the translucent membrane gently parting
seed from luscious crimson seed, albedo
soft beneath bald rind, acid juice
running down our fingers, knuckles, palms,
the mild chap of our lips from mist and flesh;
so far away from that, and still
the tangy thought of pomegranates
crowning coats-of-arms and fortress gates
like beating hearts prepared to detonate
their countless seeds across Granada,
ancient town of strangled rivers
and nameless bones in every desert hill...
In Spain, said Lorca, *the dead are more alive*
than any other place on earth. Imagine, then,
the excavation of his unmarked grave
like the quick pull on a grenade's pin,
and the sound that secrets make
as they return from that other world
of teeth and blood and fire.

Violin

Before it is seared into wood-wild rage,
a violin lives as both horse and tree.

Its treble cry holds memories of pulp
and root. Its sloped hips remember the race

through a leaf's narrow veins. Here a crow cleaned
his beak; there an owl turned its neck. Even

before music, the rosin did its work—
plugged the injured bark, froze the bugs

in place, loosened and dripped in a kiln's
rude heat, then settled into a hard pack

for the bow's slip and slur, gliss of scree,
fine stones of sound in each long hair. Wood joined

with tall oil, rosin, and steel to hold sound:
a sun above the warmed field, a wide knife's

slow release, a horse's desire for rhythm,
its pounding hooves, its deep brown ribs, its haunch

and slope. A violin almost pulls itself
apart, longing for what it was, not unlike

my father as he stood by the open mailbox,
reading my brother's first letter home.

The Wolves

Nothing satisfactory occurs in history.
—John Farmer, *Historical Memoir of Billerica*, 1812

Tonight: open windows, marshland air,
the howl of the new neighbor's dogs. One
paces and pauses in the night-blue woods;
the other licks one spot of fur until
it is an open wound.
                              Tomorrow morning
my brother will shower and dress
for the job he no longer has,
and my father will wave goodbye
from the front window. He knows
that for weeks my brother has been hiding
in the town library, waiting out the hours
until he can come home for dinner.
I imagine my brother in that musty reading room
flipping through *Basketball Digest*
and *Sports Illustrated*, avoiding the librarians
who might know my parents, and I think yes,
tonight I'll remind him about goals, money,
how our father worked with hard hands
in fish-packing plants on the wharf,
in paper-box factories in East Boston,
in a lab where no one else would touch
the chemicals. I'll tell him that his sunken eyes
remind our father of Eddie, his own brother
long dead now, the one who shot pool
as his five children hungered.
                              But I won't
say any of this. Instead, I'll log on
to the library website, wonder if my brother

is there, online too, whether our connections
will cross for a brief moment. I'll click
on John Farmer's *Historical Memoir of Billerica*
only to learn that in the summer of 1665
our town was infested with wolves. The Shawshin
joined forces with the Puritans, hunted
every last wolf, and brought the heads
to a single pile in the north of town: here,
where the dogs mourn for the blood
that holds soil and root; here,
where our parents shift and wake each night.

Linnaeus and the Patient

To cure I had to touch
    without knowing what touch
would do. I had to ease
    his trousers down and see
the mucus, shiny and constant
    on his swollen sex, the red
pustules burning to break,
    the one vein nourishing
the sickness's need. And when
    he finally lay bare, I had to percuss
the first abdomen, spleen, and liver
    of my life. I had never touched
a man this way; I had never known
    a woman. What I had learned of sex
was for plants, not men.

As I watched the base of him
    drift from one side to the other
I thought of the pepperbush
    standing as straight as physics
will permit; of the tall willows
    swaying beneath the Northern
Lights. I loved that sway,
    that drift, and the way the sex
was its own animal, unaware
    of infection glistening all around,
or whether the last woman
    had left his bed for good.
My finger glanced the tender tip
    and drew a thin thread,
tenuous, glassy, finely spun, so capable
    of breaking. But it didn't;

it stayed there, suspended between my finger
    and the man, opalescent in its shine.
I thought then of the thread
    that the Fates weave for every man,
the length upon which his life depends.
    Slowly I reached for the mercury ointment
so as not to disturb the patient, the thread,
    the sickness, and in that moment
I was certain only of this:
    that all things whirl to ruin,
and that everyone must die a little
    in order for me to cure them.

Syringe

Perhaps you've always known
her obvious thirst for more, then more:
the way she'd wish for more kissing
after the warmth of sex had risen and gone;
the way she'd beg dinner guests to stay
long after the servant had cleaned the plates
and the oil in the lamps had burned dry;
the way she always asked, even
in courtship, the *how* and the *why*
of your every declaration, wringing
the roots of thought as if the answers could
fill what existed before the pain began—
a presence that came unannounced, uninvited,
rejected at first then welcomed as part
of daily life.
        Even so, if heat is all she feels
in the throbbing, each filament a knife
of fire, a guarantee that cinders through
the night; if she wakes to weep
in the certainty of pain, its circling
through each pathway in the cheeks,
the eyes, the upper lip, so that only
the sweep of a finely woven handkerchief
can count as a kind of washing; if she
can spend all day tending to its need as if
it were the child you never had; then one day
you will have to acknowledge that she might
love the pain, and you won't be able to
imagine when or how she learned to love
anything to such excess. After
the tooth extractions have failed to relieve
the shooting; after the melancholy
has withered in her temples and refused

to leave; after you have seen the nets of nerves
unfurl in a revolt of heat; after you
and she have exhausted your search for a word
that encompasses the largeness of this woe;
remember this: the garden of lilacs
that she planted before the pain began.
Go there and see the buds clustered,
enclosed and clean, their limbs, the lean
from left to right, the dew-glistened drift
to the mulch, the blossoms that do not unfold
in time. Think *syringa vulgaris.*
Think tube, pipe, fistula. Think of filling
the barrel of the syringe, then plunging it
deep in her skin to fill the canals
of her nerves with a dark, sweet dream
of forgetting, then imagine her loving
that opposite of sense, the moment
at which the hairs of your moustache
branch into lilacs, common pinks
and blues flourishing behind her closed eyelids.
The poppy's milk has a voice
that will sing her into sleeping, and a word
for every thought as she rises
beyond the small feather bed.

On My Father's Loss of Hearing

I'd like to see more poems treat the deaf
as being abled differently, not lost
or missing something, weakened, deficient.
                    —from a listserv for the deaf

Abled differently—so vague compared
with *deaf*, obtuse but true to history,
from *deave:* to deafen, stun, amaze with noise.

Perhaps that's what we've done—amazed him
with our sorrows and complaints, the stupid jabs,
the loneliness of boredom in the house,

our wants so foreign to his own. What else
is there but loss? He's lost the sarcasm
in subtle jokes, the snarky dialogue

of British films eludes him, and phone calls
cast him adrift in that cochlear maze
that thrums and bristles even now, when

it doesn't have to: an unnecessary kind
of elegance, the vestige of a sense
no longer obligated to transmit

the crack of thawing ice that fills the yard's
wide dip in winter, or the silver scrape
of his dull rake in spring, its prongs' vibration

thrilled by grass. Imagine his desires
released like saffron pistils in the wind;
observe their trace against the cords of wood

he spent the summer splitting. See his quiet
flicker like a film, a Super-8
projected on the wall, and all of us

there, laughing on the porch without a sound.
No noisy cruelty, no baffled rage,
no aging children sullen in their lack.

Christmas in Southern California

As I watch the surfers race to the water's curl in neoprene suits
I am certain that this vision is a lie, just like the tractors

that scour the sand for fast-food wrappers and used cigarettes
and the workers who hoe desert flowers into dry soil

and the nuns, who are not a lie but are by far the most unreal,
dressed in black, their wimples starched tight, each reading

from her Bible at a cement table on the sand. Brother,
none of this is right. We are meant to burn each time we breathe,

to worry over weather reports and ice-glazed pipes, to stab
metal shovels into thigh-high banks. I would trade

this entire week of untruths for one glimpse of a sunrise
against snow. As children we coasted down a hill whose rim

was scarred with lines of balsam firs and evergreens.
In the snow's toss and swing, we leaned into the slice of speed

and threat of flight, shallow dips and hard curves,
to a target, an arrow of rough ice beyond the sun. I for one

cannot forget the singular loveliness of the cold,
its thin insult, how it made us suffer everything.

Bacalao

Each piece is a hand-sized triangle of Atlantic fish
mummified and waiting in its tiny wooden coffin

for the overnight soak, the slow simmer, the float
of flesh that rises and unfurls from its salt. Bacalao

is the mixing with boiled potatoes and garlic for the sizzle
of new life as golden fritters dipped in lemony aioli.

Bacalao is a briny delicacy, a prescription impossible
to fill in a Midwest deprived of salt, a phantom island

on a forgotten map, a dragon's tail that flails at the gate
of our strange country. It's a small thing, this need,

but what if I could put this phantom island inside me.
What if a piece could in one moment be a ghost

rising toward the legend on a map, and in another
an anchor connecting me to the sailors of Spain

and Portugal and their immigrant children whose blood
is more salt than water. Why not believe

in its lofty rise, its quick disintegration in my mouth,
and the chance to never be homesick again.

Night, Music

I was desperate for my parents, for the comfort
of a place where music was not in the wood,
rain, grass, food. After hours of practice
I spent the days' last light watching
the others from a distant hill, then followed
their frayed jeans and teased hair
to the dining hall-cum-moviehouse
for *Arsenic and Old Lace*, *Dracula*,
A Night at the Opera. After the movies
some went back to the pond's cool edge
to crack bright mints and drag
on shared cigarettes while the rest of us—
homesick, awkward—returned to the cabins
for curfew. Once, after we had climbed
into our bunks, our cabin leader opened
her cello case on the floor of the cabin.
Cello snug between two knees,
tattered sweater waddling under her arms,
she played those first vibrato groans,
each note a yearning so strong
that we didn't let our sleeping bags make
a single whisper. When she played,
it was not the beats of our hearts, it was not
the woodpecker's drumming in the trees;
the phrase was all, beyond beat or note
or bow. Even after she had drawn
her last sound, her trembling fingers could not
stop, as if she were a runner after the race, still
propelled for seconds, moments, a minute.
And then, not silence, but a kind of rest
as the bug-darkened bulb swung above her in the draft.
Then a flick of the switch, then darkness.

The Lessons

The point is this: weeks have passed
and you won't put your face in the water, won't
lie like a discarded doll on the surface,
won't hold your breath without pinching
your nose. You spend most of the time
watching band-aids loosen and cling
to the bright blue walls as boys' synthetic suits
balloon with cold water and girls'
long ponytails silken into brown ribbons.
You pretend to drift with them, all with their faces
in the water, Ben Merritt above you,
walking along the edge, bellowing
Put yaw face in the watah! like the drill
sergeant he ought to have been, and then,
because of you, *Everybody on the grass!*
and you all run, resentful and shivering
to that yard where nothing stays
clean. Hard, fat stones litter the crab grass;
a bucket's belly is stuffed with nuts and bolts;
rainwater from last weekend's storm
rots the gutters. Everyone shakes and chatters
in the dirty yard, terrified of landing
in the occasional dog droppings and the sting
of those yellow-green blades of grass
as your knees sink into sod and peat. Thumbs
angled, palms down, a smooth practice-push back
with the hand dipping down and up to the buttocks
and then the gear-like ease forward
to the imagined slap between water and air
until he is satisfied enough to say
Back to the watah! and back you go,
the refuse of his yard clinging to your feet

and hands, his pool full of twigs and acorns,
everyone but you continuing
with the Australian crawl
while you admire the skeletal rise
of flowers along the walk and wish hard
for that hour to end.
                    Finally,
playtime begins, ten minutes during which
your mother comes to get you, a relief.
But she smiles at Mr. Merritt in a way
she's never smiled at your father; she smiles at his
mottled skin and sandy hair, and her light laugh
makes her tall, young, warm. So you try it,
slip beneath the surface, let the water
hold your hair, feel the sun's slim pulse
through the watery quiet. Under water,
leaves are paws, ferns are wings,
and your mother's skirt is an orange flame
melting the sap from the pool's pine edge
as she hands the weekly check
to Mr. Merritt. You rise to catch a breath
of her, and submerge yourself again.

My Mother's Tortilla

She slices each potato thin enough
to see the light pass through its flesh. The oil
in the skillet heats until its scent
rises in a spool of smoke. I watch
her knuckles as she grasps the spatula,
pours the beaten eggs over each slice,
then, later, sweeps along the oily edge
as the tortilla blossoms in the pan.
Beyond her, the kitchen's heat dissolves
the latticework of frost that webs each pane
of glass. The branches crisp beneath the ice;
we hear the crackle, wait until their fall.
My mother inhales deeply, leans her hip
into the oven's edge. She refuses help,
the flesh of her waving like a curtain
after a long play. A few strong bones
hold her in one place—the rest are like
light spirits, growing rare and thin.
How long until she vanishes, until
the pinkish-white of each bone's glow becomes
Venetian glass, then chipped mosaic, then
dust that rises from Assyrian walls? Her spine
marks the question; she offers me a slice.

Oranges in Tissue Paper

After a painting by William J. McCloskey

Early morning, top one clothed in thin,
wrinkled white, lifted up and left for now

as others sit heavy as women, skirt
slits too high for their puckered skins

and one behind those, bright beneath what is
by now an open, swinging bulb, and to the left

another with skin flowering open, sharp
as a pinwheel, peel, zest, and papery pulp

stringing within and around the plump body,
the wedges left untouched by the servant girl

who opens just this one to see and smell,
then, remembering her mother's last kiss,

continues her morning work, a dark rush
through the cold kitchen, the idea

of oranges for everyone, Christmas
morning, delicate fragrance meeting the mist

that rises from her mouth as she races
to fill the fireplace stockings from bottom

to top with big, ripe oranges, and almost
done, plunges her fingers into one wedge

and remembers her again, dead only weeks
ago, country woman who never saw or tasted

an orange, and the girl vanishes from those
blossoms, there in the narrow oil light.

Galicia

In El Ferrol the mist is not
ffwg or *clud* or *mih*
but rootless arch, orphan blurring
the line where stonework ends

and ghosts begin. I curl my foot,
slip from the gas and drift
until the guardrail, forest, cliff
and bridge are gone; the weight

of seeing gone but for the sight
of my abuela cropped
egg-sized: black eyebrows, moustache,
jaw all thin with strain,

eyes myopic, misaligned.
Then she vanishes, and all
is blank, as if I were the space
from quill to vellum, not

nothing but evoking nothing
in a quiver of white.
Or an *ellipsis*, from the Greek:
to leave out, to fall short.

The Lonely Bitters

Without you here, everything's askew—
the porch's chairs fall down, their plastic new
to city soot, old rain, and fallen sparks
from last week's sulfur-heavy fireworks.

I find a greasy stain on every shirt;
everything I cook seems spoiled or burnt,
and even reading isn't right. I dropped
the *Norton* and its pages flurried, stopped:

"Their Lonely Betters," Auden's lovely lines
on silence, animals, and human signs;
but instead I saw "The Lonely Bitters," thought
of the Angosturas in your cabinet,

the darkened bottle, scent of gentian root,
quassia chips and licorice, and I could
almost see you mix your favorite drink:
whiskey, vermouth, a bitter dash, the clink

of ice in the shaker, then the steady pour.
Unlucky bitters, malaria's failed cure—
perhaps they miss the thrill of your approach,
your quiet gaze, your affectionate touch.

While Reading Ovid's *Amores*

Emerging from in between two leaves
of porous, yellowed paper:
a hair not so unlike the ones
Juno used to shed all around
the old house. The tome's hand-oiled
edges and odor of mold suggest
years of unreading, years
that this single unyielding cat hair
has managed to hang on. Perhaps
on a breezy day—I like to imagine
sometime in 1968—a reader left
this book on his couch to go
for a walk, and in his absence
his cat rubbed its ear against the pages.
A book of poems is never the same
as love, but a cat doesn't look for that.
Its search is for a memory
that will last until the next morning,
when it can wake and find
the one object in the house
that nuzzles back.

In one poem, Ovid chastises his lover:
I told you to stop using that rinse,
And now you've no hair left to tint.
Dear Juno, cozy to table legs
and doorways, licker of lead chips
that flaked along the well-grooved
window pane, I wonder: how much
of your hair is left now?
I'll remember you as you were:
a hairy, lewd Roman, lounging

and eating paint as if from a platter,
staring me down with a look that said
you have to earn your grave.

The Griffin

For George Herbert, thinking meant feeling;
    a sermon on the complexities of predestination

was as exciting as a country girl sitting in the front pew.
    I learned this lesson best years ago

from a tutor in England who met with me each Tuesday.
    Her last name was Griffin, which was, I thought,

the most interesting thing about her.
    Our meetings were dismal for both of us:

I thought rhymed poetry was a bore
    and she kept squinting toward the tiny desk clock

for the minute she could be alone again. One afternoon,
    after several like this, she must have decided

that reading aloud could help. She cleared her throat,
    adjusted her giant glasses, opened to "The Collar,"

and read. With her Cornish lilt, she lingered
    over *Shall I ever sigh and pine?* as if it were

her own question, and by the time she got to
    Is the year only lost to me? she seemed to have forgotten

Herbert, and me, altogether. I saw a struggle in her,
    heard a tightening in her throat, then a gasp

after she uttered the final words, and then
    she nearly left the prison of her body, her tears

revealing that she really was part lion, part eagle.
    How often have I read Herbert's poem in the years since,

only to hear the unexplained weeping, and the choler
    that bound the griffin, even as she flexed her wings.

Winter Storm, 1st Avenue

A small bird stands regnant on the sill
haloed by the darkest light of the year.
With stems and stalks he crowds a hollow
between the building's bricks, a rough nest
dressed with frozen droppings in thin lines.
Beyond him, cars scuttle like bugs
through dirt and salt; a shopkeeper
arranges blue vases and orange flowers;
the clock above the drugstore reads 8 a.m.;
steam from the bagel shop and laundromat
mixes then smells the same; garbage bags
sealed with tape puddle in the road;
an empty bottle rests alone
beneath the roof's barbed wire.
And for the first time ever, the window
across the way frames a woman,
head lowered to read a book
in the blue cloud-light, the pages covered
with colored paper slips. She brings
a thoughtful finger to her mouth,
turns on one foot, then walks away
to show white cotton briefs
and the elusive swing
of her smooth, pale legs.

My Father's Radio

He listened behind the unfinished pyramid of broken wood
while checking for mites and spiders. Saturday afternoons,

hours of Frank Sinatra, Tony Bennett, Big Joe Williams,
men garbling ads for Giant Glass and for Tony Floramo's

restaurant in Chelsea—where, as Bill Marlowe noted,
The meat falls off the bone! Silver sounds died as dust fizzled

in the speaker's holes, old grass smelled up the cowhide handle,
green loam dried its cloth-fine threads.

Sweatshirt lacquered with sap and oil, he'd swing
the radio onto the heap of weeds in the green wheelbarrow

and listen as he clipped the border brush crusted with thorns.
He listened to official news updates while he sharpened

his worn saws and clippers, as he sprayed bee hives
then watched their paper lanterns drift down

onto the pine needles. Their own music was vacant, abstract,
then silenced against traffic reports and weather watches.

He listened in that place where he disposed of everything—
the marshland beyond our steps narrow as a trough,

encircled with whorls of lady slippers. He listened as he brought
his offerings—wrinkled peat moss bags fattened with wet leaves,

birch branches peeling like snakes, rocks and pebbles
from the neighbor's yard. I watched him from the bathroom,

the kitchen, the swing set he built on the pine needles,
and he never looked up to smile or wave, so focused

was he on the task at hand, the radio leaning
against the house, or fastened to his leather belt.

Mendeleev

He knows that oxygen is a mistake, that magnesium
    holds the eye of every flower to the sun, and that,
        in some regions, rain ignites and burns. So how

can you blame him if he spends the night sweeping
    columns of cards away for single kings
        to rest alone until they find their match? This is one

pattern that soothes—the feel of the cards slipping
    through his fingers, candle burning low beside
        a greasy glass of beer. He shuffles the gray edges

into lovely three-card spills, the chance for a bond
    between red and black, highest to lowest, hanging
        one beneath the next. He lingers over one bad hand,

studies the blue whirls on the back of each card,
    and in that moment of sleeplessness, he can almost see
        his own name written in cursive, then atoms

spinning like bees. Later he thought of something
    snapping, a simple falling leaf that with its grace
        marked time in the universe. If you told me years ago

that today I'd read a book about valences, bonds, and shells,
    I wouldn't have believed you. But now I see landscapes
        and kingdoms, elements dancing in a single spiral

of light. Beyond my book, the goldenrod blooms
    in plume-like clusters along the broken fence.
        In a few days, our neighbor will come over

to our side and offer to shear the bush and Heidi will say
    yes, that's fine, thanks. Until then the yellowed branches
        will swell and dip, shadow the eggplant and tomato

seedlings, cool the hay that Heidi has strewn all over
    the new wet mulch. They will reach up and out,
        nearly break from their corset, and live.

Later tonight, I will think of Mendeleev as I arrange
    my foundations, tidy up my tableau. Corset. Bloom. Valence.
        I used to bring my notebook everywhere with hopes

of catching a word or phrase before it left the world.
    I thought it meant something, saving all those
        vanishings, but what good did it do? Hours with pen

suspended above paper, waiting for a word that no one
    could touch or taste. Now I just break out a pack
        of fresh cards and fall into the trance. I believed

that this would bring me to the wilderness where poetry
    lives, but instead the cards replaced that need for loss
        and breaking, and now it's gone, perhaps for good.

Real Jardín Botánico, Madrid

And then, more eye-brightening roses, each head a swell
    of petals, supernumerous, frail, purpled, pinked, and grooved,
        the favorite flower of every civilization, the scatter of which

plumes across my sandals and skirt, and when I look above
    I see each overhead trellis a haunted house of near-chaos:
        the saucer-white Mermaid remontant, one bloom per season

simply not enough; the drift of Crepuscules blousy and obscene
    in their looseness, dangerous reminders of detachment;
        and yes, more myrtle trees flaring in the too-slow breeze,

their branches indiscriminate but firm; more juniper trees,
    spread wide and low, each cone full of medicine, the Houdini
        of the garden squeezed into impossibility. Amid this
        commotion

and the fury of the heat, I see an española checking
    her reflection in a pink compact. At first she touches her hair
        and cheek, then reaches for the comb in her purse, and it is

a quiet moment amidst the Noisettes and thorns, or noiseless,
    at least, and private. But then in the light of those flowers,
        in the too-dense sway of fragrance, her body begins its
        betrayal:

the hand that moves to her chest, the sunken shadow
    on her skin, and then the lurch that nearly sends her
        from the narrow bench. She tilts her head toward a corner

of empty soil, leans over and surrenders to what her stomach
    will not tolerate, and then, when done, raises a dark cloth
        to her burning face, just as her novio comes to hold the
        small

of her back and the loose black curls on her neck, glistening now
and baby-fine. He is a little amazed at her face, which
may not be like the one she makes when she is crying.

Her face says   *it would be simple   more fragrant*
   if eros were its own clean end
         but there is no such ending in desire

My Grandfather on Roosevelt Island

Metropolitan Hospital, 1933

The scene is still preserved as if just left:
a smuggled bottle of whiskey, amber liquid
heavy with dust, a half-filled cup on the wash basin,
its porcelain brown with cracks, a teabag
dried and clinging to its edge. In the sun that fades
the plastic irises and daisies, he's almost there,
in that room, the grandfather who died
in a sanitarium hundreds of miles from here,
work clothes draped on his frame, dry skull
free of flesh, dark flowers blooming
in the eye sockets, his open jaw revealing
the teeth of the wolf that orphaned his children,
white bones cleaved and bursting
from the rusted cuffs that held him to the bed,
each chafed hoop an eye.
                                    But it is easy
to think of this and then see other eyes
everywhere—of old women who scratched
their faces for viruses and nerves, of worms'
ocilli twisting purple in the grave-deep soil,
of peacock grass molting with rot, of swine
buried where they once grazed,
and whole empty hospitals warehousing eyes
of lost criminals, the insane, the tubercular,
sweet and ignorant of rules, broken eyeglass frames
crushed and melted into the asphalt.
Even strewn clothing is furnished with eyes:
buttons, sequins, leprosy, and worse. The eyes
of branches graft onto others, cherry becomes
maple becomes rows of shoots now dead
but still with eyes.

                    I know there is shame
in his death: the extinct illness, the neglected,
far-off room, the unmarked grave. A kind
of pulse still beats through him;
wristwatches choked and broken with dust
watch my hands for some sign.

Poem for a New Apartment

Let your new space ripen
like the berries that sit
in your refrigerator—
cool, blue, heavy. See the glass
bowl on your table, how it marks
time, its spare light caught in the door
frame's speckled paint. Look
to the oily ships and barges
beneath your ledge, sluggish
with autumn cold. Notice the floor's
dark grain weave a bay—no, a river—
of reflection, and somewhere
beyond this place an inlet, then an ocean
wide with shine, crowded
with fish, their light fins
sweeping the current. I saw
them move. I know.

Katydid

After Neruda

Katydids are proof that no living being, however minute
or common, is happy with its home. Millions thrive

on bark and waxy leaves, but their trembling steps
are those of children new to walking. They are most

ambitious in flight, not so unlike Octave Chanute, who,
with his grand dreams of small insects created a gliding machine

called the katydid, and on a strip of Indiana sand rose for a brief,
faltering moment before his many-winged contraption drifted

to the dunes. Perhaps the katydid is as daring and restless
as Octave Chanute. Just consider its name, which mimics

its strident call. *Katy did, she did* creaks from its forewings
up to the highest branches and down into caves,

a brazen declaration inscrutable to those who sleep
on tidy mattresses, under roofs. What is that sound, we wonder.

Is it pen on paper? Or two forks singing? No, it is the katydid,
the sound of which is the composite of all changeful things.

Moon Jellies

I lost him twice today: once
in the glide from kiss to burn
when, like Daphne, he seemed to race
toward wildwood, undone;

a desperate run toward trees and grass,
a slender shade of sleep
that when he woke still traced his skin
like whorls of laurel, deep

and fine. And later, in the cool
aquarium, beyond
anemones, belugas, tangs,
beyond the rigid fronds

of coral reefs: jellyfish, moon
jellies behind a wall
of hand-thick glass. Beneath the blue
gels of light, their shawls

of nerves fluoresced as pink
four-chambered stars; their rims
a sway of glass-blue hairs. No need
to sting, the drift of slim

non-bodies floating up, their trace
more pulse than presence, more
quintessence than glass case. Just then
I noticed his calm stare,

then purple rapture, a trance unlike
any human state
and then his body crossed the glass
to gently undulate

among that prehistoric crowd,
no name or eyes or skin,
no weight of human color, just
the ceaseless drift toward bliss.

Clarinet

Every time someone peels an orange
  something tears in me
as I remember the smell
  of peels lingering in that velvet case,
their humidity staying
  in the wood long after drying
into forgotten skins. Then
  the reeds, how the knife would lift
a thin dust from top and edge
  of cut cane, the thin stick
of green bamboo pressing
  the warped white edge into roundness,
how rubbing the back of the reed
  with newsprint sealed the pores,
made it ring, and how fine,
  when finished, the pleasure
of rubbing oily thumb against the grain
      in my pocket
          in autumn rain
until, in the light again, each pulp heart
  glowed and spread with touch
of tongue to fiber, silky threads
  vanishing in movement, burn of hot wind
spinning through wood and spring, vein
  and bore, beads of condensation
curing the ebony's openness.

I forgot how many times
  it brought me to that burning light,
that spinning wheel, but tonight
  in the shower, before
our guests arrived, I pressed my ear
  to your narrow back and heard the rain—

the singular, metronomic beat,
    the legato hum of your voice breaking
the cylinder of your body.

Flamenco

In a public square swollen
with flowers and canopies,
on a night whose wrists
are ribboned with heat,
the guitarrista sits on church steps
and thirsts for sound.

His song is a flamingo
one pink leg poised,
an immigrant running back home,
a peasant imprisoned in song,
and it speaks, says

if he touches me just once
with his mouth
his fingers
with the echoes
of what he will not do—
if he touches me—

and you hope that one night is enough
to unwind the root of him,
but it will not stop speaking:

> *pull at his neck*
> *pull him down*

for a picture
of this hunger

> *for a moment*
> *of pure vanishing*

Love Poem

I was the warmth that lifted
from your pilled sheets, the glow
of Sebastian in the picture book
of saints, the moon gliding
through the window beside your bed.

I was the clock in your kitchen
waiting to catch you in my gears.
In the TV, I was the blue tube
that saw your sadness run as silt
down a mountain. I was the rush
in the vein of every oak leaf
that crowded your window.

I was the drift of you before your edges
twisted into a man. The swing
of your loose pant cuff. The joint
in the threshold; the rusted cart
behind the house. You sensed

a visitor, but how can I say
that I was the one who curled
the wallpaper and held the model
airplane in its place? That it was I
late at night, running in the current
of your clock radio, searching
the seashell of your ear?

Afternoon, Córdoba

Not the body as a clock
    or wheel
        or hydraulic rush
    or cocked gun
but how much the body can do
without the mind: the salty joint
    and bone, the want and lean
toward lime-scented shave and pomade
    in still-wet hair,
the body gliding toward every muscle and falling
from all learned things for one taste
of the fine row of hairs along abdomen
and limbs pulsing with light.
    It seems so easy
    for the mind to vanish
        in a narrow switch
that begins its journey in the hot slip
of afternoon
    but the switch never ends:
it is a hovering, an incompletion
as the mind returns to its ghost.

Flu, Umpqua Lighthouse Park, Oregon

When you are well, you are:
thin bones, feather skin, bird toes,
bird love. But I cannot bear it
when you are sick. This time
it was in May, in a yurt with green canvas
pulled tight against latticed wood.
Outside, the brush swarmed
and almost swallowed us
as you swelled heavy with heat,
thick-tongued, your damp skin
an empty brown glass.

I left you shifting and coughing
in that tight screw of a sleeping bag,
sealed the lip of the yurt, forced
the rented car's wheels into the muddle
of needles and rocks.
I hurried to the nearest diner
and asked the kind waitress
for oatmeal. As she scooped
the porridge into a styrofoam cup
I stared at tables wet with tea and jelly,
at healthy customers sitting up to eat.
When I returned, I wiped the sweat
from your chest and arms
and lay beside you to spoon
the hot oatmeal into your partly
opened mouth. Why, as I lifted
your head, did I feel so close
to that rim of light before the star,
that ring of heat around the heart?
Why was I certain

that I had inherited something
from you, almost was you, enough
to whisper *Lover. Brother. Son. Mine.*

Inside Sleep

Be it the faint blue light
that recedes from your skin
or the waking of your angles
each morning, I am still unused
to you, as drowsy reefs
to the sun's planished glint,
as the yellow pine needles
to their dignified, autumnal end.
Here now I lie beside you
and I ache as if
the miles that once separated us
were still a stubborn line
of dull earth tracing itself in me.
Some nights, your chest no broader
than my own, you heave as though
moving great weight, arms spindled
in an urgent grasp as cold wind
sucks at the curtains, even if
the windows are clasped shut.
Inside sleep, infinite longing.

Farmer, Middlesex Canal, 1810

The canal is a hollow reed
a jointed fissure
each knot a wooden lock
to be fastened then released
to the lurch and sigh
of its most ancient sound
qanah   qanah

The canal is a bank where asters
blossom and break
and in their breaking a memory
of what came before:
my father's flute
resting in its pouch by the fire

my mother's cane
and the echo of its tapping

my fishing rod from childhood
the hook a rusted curl
from hours of dipping

and in the watery wind
my wife's distant breath
yes, she: a narrow flute
a slender road
a small beauty
that required close watching

She is there in each new hook
in the ice that fractures stone
I know the canal's flow is the remnant
of a certain kind of brilliance
a ruthless optimism ringing in the night

Elotes

When I walk all day on days like this
I become pure yearning
for the golden wands
of chile powder and crunch that glow
beneath makeshift awnings all over
the city. Today I wait for the abuelita
serving cobs from her front stoop,
for the lingering threads of husk to whisker
green as the corn emerges from the cauldron
of roiling water, for the flecks of queso
to melt between kernels and glisten down
my wrist, for the butter to thin and swirl
in my mouth and through my veins,
turning my blood the color of milk.
Between that first bite and the abuelita's
slow turn toward the kitchen,
her steps on the worn, speckled tiles
become my grandmother's
in her last days as she beat water rats
to death beside the stove
and the gingham trim of her apron
becomes the hush and swing
of the apron that lingers in the back
of my closed broom closet.

Chicago, 1950

After a photograph by Harry Callahan

Twelve years is a long time to wait
for a gelatin print of winter trees
that has no reason to be.

Maybe he always stopped right before
his best one; maybe he took the bus
to Lake Michigan every day for six months

hoping to find the perfect light
in the thin branches. Maybe each time
he was about to start his second roll

he stopped, having come so close
to that ineluctable brilliance, hoping
he could feel that warmth again.

Perhaps on this day, the day he took
Chicago, 1950, he thought of what
didn't belong to him—so many things

beyond trees and snow: the bare light
on the corner of Montrose and Kenmore,
the lake swelling into floes

of night ice, black water, dark wind,
the narrow pier that, with its string
for a rail, was more absence than presence.

Perhaps it was then that he remembered reading
about the old man from Provence, who for years
had traveled from one village to another

with his portable projector, showing
silent films to anyone who would watch them.
He would set his projector on a card table,

spool the nitrate reel into the sprockets,
and lecture until the film's quickened pulse
came to an end. This in the mountains

of Provence, in 1950: beauty offered
again and again, even when no one
asked for it. Perhaps for that moment,

the bare trunks and branches became shadows,
but not shadows—objects in space that had no
comparison to any living thing. And he took them.

Pre-Cana

We start with simple things—who will iron,
who will pay the bills. I watch one couple
hold hands and another cross and uncross their legs.
Then come worksheets: *revengeful or forgiving?*
Perceptive or unobservant? One woman pulls
at her nametag, smudges her handwriting.
Outside, children skate on Frog Pond,
their blades stuttering into well-worn grooves.
Protesters clutter the Common with pamphlets
and bullhorns, and the Shaw monument endures
another thankless afternoon.
                                        After we've marked
our checks and circles, after the warm push
of embarrassment that comes with talk of sex
in front of any priest, we close our eyes
and breathe deeply to imagine our lives together
in five years, twenty-five, fifty. Frog Pond
vanishes into the clouds and I feel a pressure,
a memory of the ones who hung as heretics
near this room, who came to Boston
again and again, as if they loved the knife
that cut each ear away, as if the swing and heat
of the noose would feel good. And in that moment
of musing, his every goodness—
the photographs that reach like hands,
the gestures that carry small music—
is gone. I sketch words on my blank page
but his pencil's rush stops my swinging limbs.
I look at his notepad:

> *garden*
> *travel*
> *curious*
> *affection*

His heart's tight fist drowns the room in sun. He reads my list—

> *old bones*
> *pink pills*
> *forgetting*

and in his calm, singular glance, I know
he will burn the heretic out of me.

A Classroom in the New Talbot School, circa 1910

After an anonymous photo in the Billerica Museum

Today's lesson was about the Big Dipper,
the seven stars that with their distant ring
are always ready to slice the frozen skirts
of cloud, the whirl of errant rocks
spooling through the sky, darkness itself. Tucked
away in this classroom, these children seem blind,

their faces blurred and stunned as blinds
on the windows stripe each cheek. Perhaps the dipper
that immersed the negative slipped and stuck
to the emulsion; maybe each blurred ring
is a zephyr of forgetting that will rock
each child to sleep after the nanny's skirt

rustles down the hall tonight. But this fantasy skirts
around another story; indeed, every photo blinds
us to what's beyond its borders. Consider the massive rocks
in the river, the power of the current as it dips
into the mill, the speed of the small hands in a ring
of loose wool threads, sweat, and smoke. The tucks

and ruffles in this photo might have been tucked
by mill girls, their work concealed by the skirt
of trees and the ghostly ring
of the river's rising mist. The girls are blind
to distraction, focused only on the dipper's
release of dye, the loud pounding of the turbines, the rock

of the tireless jennies. And you cannot see the rocky
path behind the school where, inside a moist tuck
of peat and grass, a sickened dipper

bird has come to die. The river's oily skirt
is cluttered with dozens blinded
with the taste of bitter glue, opalescent rings

of too-sweet tanner, their final treble ring
unknown to us. Today, only the rocks
by the mill remain, and the memory of blinds
closed to a pain that was paid for, a ghost in the tuck
of every hem and weave that we skirt
to this day. If sometime you see this photo, dip

beneath the platinum, look beyond the ring of schoolchildren
to see the makers of their tucked skirts, mill girls hardened by rocks,
and the stillness of dippers after their blind flailing.

Daguerreotype, 1848

On the top edge, in faded scratches:
E. White, Maker. Finest Quality. NY.
Smooth copper backs the plate,
its four corners clipped
at forty-five degrees,
the upper left one crimped
from pincers grabbing its edges.

And the man—unnamed, confused,
a young American officer
with an ill-fitted frock coat.
Notice his sword, its visible hilt,
the handle a tasseled Phrygian cap
with a four-sided ivory grip.
See how it curls like a blade
into his hands,
                already gone…but not
really gone. That's how it works:
in this medium, whatever moves
vanishes.
            Like his eyes—
unfortunate, almost crossed
as if he stumbled in front
of the camera, in front of death to say
I've never done the thing I wanted in all my life.

Plaza de Toros, Bilbao

It's just the right amount of suffering:
the bull's already punch-drunk at the gate,
haunches buckling, furious with weight
of swollen scrotum, swinging bowels, sting
of picas driven deep into his neck.
With pink muleta flowering in the sand,
the matador turns once. His slender hands
seduce the bull towards the ice-filled truck
that idles for the toro's bloodied corpse.
It's just the right amount—the cigar smoke,
small trumpets bleating, women selling beer—
to forget the spray of Franco's bombs, the lisp
rumbling against and through the common folk,
collaboration fouling sweet night air.

Reenactment, Gettysburg

Midsummer. Blood-red clouds. The sky
a cave of hot stars, white with distance.
Beyond the motor lodge, the sandy road
takes the shape of a long animal curled
in sleep. Fruit bats lisp in the branches;
I can count them from our bed.

Tonight I think of the heat that haloed
each soldier, of the cannon's long tremble
against the parched grass, and how,
at Pickett's Charge, I found myself
almost wanting clots of blood
to gel and glisten on the men's
woolen uniforms, to stick in the folds
of their wet necks. Then, in the sun
that sent me spinning, how the *almost*
became exact, entire, a need
to see the doctor dress their wounds
and watch for when the yellow beads
of pus would rise from every man
into a hope of healing, how wild
I was with wanting as I imagined him
fingering the ooze from one gash
to the next, a salve that promised
the men to their thumb-shaped tombs.

I wonder how you can sleep
with the smell of bleach on the motel
towels, mites in the dimpled sheets,
the memory of the dead, the ease
with which I might lift your narrow bones.
I watch you twitch and breathe
until the blinds brindle the new sun.

Epigram for the Boston Accent

After Martial

My voice will carry you to a paradise of prigs
where men don't leave and women say
A cracked dish never breaks. You'll hear
the rough edge of a nation, see the palsied finger
that lures all of us back. Perhaps to you
I sound low, uncouth, but don't mistake
the dropped *r* for ignorance. Instead,
imagine a people stiff as shingles,
stunned by snow and constant salt.
Hear in every word the work it takes
to stay alive.   *Ah.   Ah.*

Notes

"Granada": Lorca was assassinated during the Spanish Civil War and was buried in a mass grave in 1936.

"Linnaeus and the Patient": Though Carl Linnaeus is best known for his taxonomic system of nomenclature for plants, he was a physician for a brief time as a young man, and treated mostly venereal diseases of servants in the village.

"Syringe": "In 1853, Charles Gabriel Pravaz and Alexander Wood developed the first syringe with a needle fine enough to pierce the skin…The first recorded fatality from a hypodermic-syringe-induced overdose was Dr. Wood's wife. The tragedy arose because she was injecting morphine to excess." (from the Utopian Surgery website)

"While Reading Ovid's *Amores*": Ovid's lines come from the Guy Lee translation of *Amores*. The final line was one found in one of Kafka's notebooks after his death.

"Plaza de Toros, Bilbao": During the Spanish Civil War (1936-39) the civilian town of Guernica was bombed by Nazi planes acting under General Franco's orders.

"Reenactment, Gettysburg": Civil War doctors believed that the appearance of pus on a wound meant that the wound was healing, when in fact it was a sign of infection. Doctors often spread the pus from one man onto another; within days, both men would be dead.

"Epigram for the Boston Accent": During his visit to Boston, Oscar Wilde referred to the city as a "paradise of prigs."

Acknowledgments

Grateful acknowledgement is made to the publications in which the following poems first appeared:

32 Poems: "While Reading Ovid's *Amores*" and "Christmas in Southern California"
Barely South Review: "The Griffin"
Cimarron Review: "The Lessons"
Crab Orchard Review: "My Grandfather on Roosevelt Island"
Grand Street: "Reenactment, Gettysburg"
Greensboro Review: "The Wolves"
Gulf Stream: "Poem for a New Apartment"
Karamu: "Night, Music"
Louisiana Literature: "My Father's Radio"
Madison Review: "Granada" and "Flamenco"
Missouri Review: "Afternoon, Córdoba," "Linnaeus and the Patient," "Moon Jellies," and "Syringe"
Notre Dame Review: "Mendeleev"
Poetry International: "Winter Storm, 1ˢᵗ Avenue"
Prairie Schooner: "Violin"
Quarterly West: "Chicago, 1950"
Quercus Review: "Bacalao," "Elotes," and "Real Jardín Botánico, Madrid"
Seattle Review: "The Lonely Bitters"
Southern Review: "Epigram for the Boston Accent," "Oranges in Tissue Paper," "On My Father's Loss of Hearing"

The author wishes to thank the New York Times Foundation, the Illinois Arts Council, and the National Endowment for the Arts for their support.

The text and display type were set in Adobe Jenson, a faithful electronic version of the 1470 roman face of Nicolas Jenson. Jenson was a Frenchman employed as the mintmaster at Tours. Legend has it that he was sent to Mainz in 1458 by Charles VII to learn the new art of printing in the shop of Gutenberg, and import it to France. But he never returned, appearing in Venice in 1468; there his first roman types appeared, in his edition of Eusebius. He moved to Rome at the invitation of Pope Sixtus IV, where he died in 1480.

Type historian Daniel Berkeley Updike praises the Jenson Roman for "its readability, its mellowness of form, and the evenness of color in mass." Updike concludes, "Jenson's roman types have been the accepted models for roman letters ever since he made them, and, repeatedly copied in our own day, have never been equalled." The display type used for the title on the front and back cover is Legato. The author's name is set in Classica on the front cover. Adobe Jensen was used for the back cover text.

Silverfish Review Press is committed to preserving ancient forests and natural resources. We elected to print *The Lessons* on 30% post consumer recycled paper, processed chlorine free. As a result, for this printing, we have saved: 1 tree (40' tall and 6-8" diameter), 499 gallons of water, 293 kilowatt hours of electricity, 64 pounds of solid waste, and 120 pounds of greenhouse gases. Thomson-Shore, Inc. is a member of Green Press Initiative, a nonprofit program dedicated to supporting authors, publishers, and suppliers in their efforts to reduce their use of fiber obtained from endangered forests. For more information, visit www.greenpressinitiative.org.

Cover design by Valerie Brewster, Scribe Typography.
Text design by Rodger Moody and Connie Kudura, ProtoType Graphics.
Printed on acid-free papers and bound by Thomson-Shore, Inc.